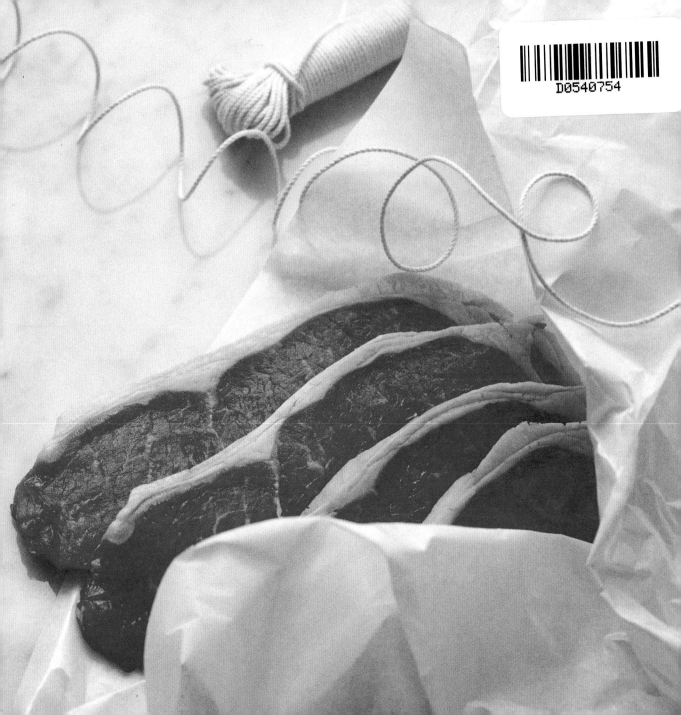

steak

steak

Fiona Beckett photography by Martin Brigdale

RYLAND
PETERS
& SMALL

LONDON NEW YORK

First published in the
United Kingdom in 2006
by Ryland Peters & Small
20–21 Jockey's Fields
London WC1R 4BW
www.rylandpeters.com

10 9 8 7 6 5 4 3 2 1

ISBN-10: 1 84597 207 4
ISBN-13: 978 1 84597 207 3

A CIP record for this book is available
from the British Library.

Dedication
For my boys. Steak heaven.

Senior Designer Steve Painter
Commissioning Editor Julia Charles
Editors Sharon Cochrane and
      Rachel Lawrence
Production Gemma Moules
Art Director Anne-Marie Bulat
Publishing Director Alison Starling

Food Stylist Sunil Vijayakar
Props Stylist Helen Trent

Acknowledgements
Thanks first and foremost to the
suppliers of the exceptional steak I used
for this book – the excellent Aberdeen-
based on-line butcher, Donald Russell
(www.donaldrussell.com), who
specializes in grass-fed Scottish beef;
Pampas Plains (www.pampasplains.com),
which supplies fabulous-tasting
Argentinian meat; and my local butcher,
Joe Collier of Eastwood Butchers in
Berkhamsted, Hertfordshire. (Tel: 01442
865012). What Joe doesn't know about
steak isn't worth knowing. Thanks too to
the team at RPS who finally gave in and
let me write this book – particularly to
Commissioning Editor Julia Charles, my
copy editors, Sharon Cochrane and
Rachel Lawrence, and designer Steve
Painter – and to photographer Martin
Brigdale, one of the best in the business.

The publisher would like to thank
Lidgates Butchers of Holland Park,
London.

Notes
• All spoon measurements are level
unless otherwise specified.
• All eggs are large unless otherwise
specified. Uncooked or partly cooked
eggs should not be served to the
very young, the very old, those with
compromised immune systems or
to pregnant women.

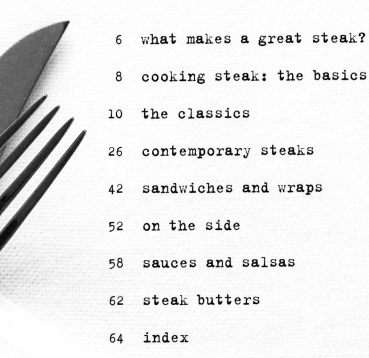

contents

what makes a great steak?

For me, steak is the ultimate fast food – easy to cook and a treat at any time. However, the difference between a good steak and a great one undoubtedly lies in the quality of the meat you use.

The best steak comes from a breed specifically reared for top-quality beef production, such as Aberdeen Angus, Hereford, Limousin or Charolais, or for the world's most expensive beef – Japanese Wagyu.

Cattle that are reared as naturally as possible will produce the best beef. They should be fed on grass during the summer, as they are on Argentina's famous pampas, and on hay and cereal-based feeds during the winter. They should also be reared slowly in order for the meat to develop the rich marbling of fat that gives a deep flavour.

Good-quality beef comes from butchers or meat suppliers that age their meat properly. It comes from carcasses that have been hung for at least 2 weeks – preferably 3–4 weeks – rather than joints that have been vacuum-packed. A good butcher will cut steaks evenly and to the thickness you require.

A great steak does not necessarily come from the most expensive cuts. Meltingly tender and delicious though cuts such as fillet and sirloin are, there are many lesser cuts that make fantastic meals, as thrifty French cooks know well. Just try the delicious Bavette aux Echalotes (page 12) or the tasty Char-grilled Steak Fajitas (page 51). Steak can also be stretched by using less and cutting it thinly, a method often used in Asian dishes, such as Thai-style Steak and Tomato Salad (page 39) and Vietnamese Pho (page 40).

Good steak has a natural affinity with good wine. It's the natural partner for the best red wines in the world, especially Bordeaux, the wines of the Northern Rhone area, top-quality Tuscan reds, and Cabernet and Shiraz from the premier vineyards of the new world. What better with steak than a good wine-based sauce like the classic Entrecôte Marchand de Vin (page 11)?

If you're a steak lover, as I am, I hope this book will help you to make your favourite steak dishes taste even better and give you some new ideas for enjoying these most-prized cuts of meat.

cooking steak: the basics

The individual recipes in the book will guide you through the steps you need to follow to get the best results, but there are a few general pointers that are helpful to bear in mind.

✱ Always start with your steak at room temperature. If it's straight from the refrigerator, the short cooking time in some of the recipes could leave the centre of the meat cold.

✱ Trim off any visible fat. Most steaks are cooked too quickly to cook the fat through and your guests will probably want to cut it off anyway.

✱ Pat the meat dry with kitchen paper before cooking so that it will brown, particularly if it has been vacuum-packed or stored in a plastic bag. Even if you have marinated the steak beforehand, dry it before you cook it or it will simmer rather than sizzle.

✱ If you are frying steak, make sure the frying pan is hot before you begin. A ridged stove-top grill pan should be very hot. However, if you are frying in oil and butter or cooking a steak coated in peppercorns or a spicy rub, you will need to reduce the heat slightly as these could catch and burn if the temperature is too high. When cooking on a ridged stove-top grill pan or a barbecue, oil the steak rather than the pan or rack.

✱ Always rest your steak, lightly covered, on a warm plate for at least 3 minutes after cooking. I can't stress how important this is, as it results in a much more tender, juicier steak.

how long should you cook a steak?

This depends how thick the steak is and how well cooked you like it. Most of the steaks in the book are cooked medium-rare or rare, which is how I find most people prefer them. I know a few hardened carnivores who like their steaks 'blue' – simply shown the pan and barely cooked at all – but, apart from Carpaccio (page 31), I don't think that suits most steak dishes. If you prefer your steak medium to well done, simply add a minute or two to the cooking times in the recipes.

the classics

One of the great French classics, Entrecôte Marchand de Vin (wine merchant's steak) is cooked in a simple red wine sauce. I say simple, but I actually think it's worth using a seriously good wine and drinking the rest of the bottle with it. It's usually made with red Bordeaux, but I like to use a good, but not too oaky, syrah or shiraz.

entrecôte marchand de vin

2 entrecôte or sirloin steaks, 225 g each and 2 cm thick

1 tablespoon olive oil

40 g butter, softened

2 shallots, very finely chopped

125 ml good-quality red wine, such as Bordeaux, syrah or shiraz

2 rounded tablespoons finely chopped flat leaf parsley

sea salt and freshly ground black pepper

to serve

sautéed potatoes or Smooth, Creamy Mash (page 53)

a mixed leaf salad

serves 2

Trim the steaks of any excess fat and pat dry with kitchen paper. Heat a heavy frying pan over medium to high heat for about 2 minutes. Add the olive oil and, when it is hot, add 15 g of the butter. Wait until the foaming subsides, then put the steaks in the pan. Cook for 3 minutes, then turn and cook for another 2–3 minutes for a medium-rare steak. Transfer to a warm plate and cover lightly with aluminium foil.

Discard the fat in the pan and add half the remaining butter. Once it has melted, add the shallots and cook over low heat for about 2 minutes. Increase the heat, pour in the wine and let bubble away for 2–3 minutes until it has reduced by about two-thirds. Gradually whisk in the remaining butter, pour in any juices that have accumulated under the steak and stir. Season with salt and pepper, then add the parsley.

Serve the steaks with the sauce poured over, accompanied by sautéed or mashed potatoes and a mixed leaf salad.

Bavette or skirt steak is one of the most popular French bistro cuts. It needs to be cooked quickly otherwise it can be tough, but if you buy well-aged cuts of beef, it has the most fabulous, intense flavour.

bavette aux échalotes

2 tablespoons olive oil

350 g well-aged, thinly sliced bavette (skirt steak)

25 g butter

350 g even-sized shallots, quartered

75 ml red wine vinegar

75 ml Simple Steak Sauce (see below) or beef stock

sea salt and freshly ground black pepper

to serve

Smooth, Creamy Mash (page 53) or Classic French Fries (page 53)

green salad (optional)

serves 2

Heat a cast-iron frying pan over medium heat for 5 minutes until almost smoking. Trickle a little of the olive oil over each side of the meat, rub it in and season lightly with salt and pepper. Add the meat to the pan and fry for 1½–2 minutes on each side, depending on whether you want it rare or medium-rare, pressing the pieces down firmly with a wooden spatula. Transfer to a warm plate and cover lightly with aluminium foil.

Wipe the pan clean with kitchen paper, then heat for a couple of minutes. Add the remaining olive oil and half the butter and, once melted, fry the shallots for 6–7 minutes until well browned. Add the vinegar and let bubble up until almost evaporated. Add the simple steak sauce, the remaining butter and any juices that have accumulated under the meat and heat through. Taste and adjust the seasoning, if necessary.

Serve the steak with the shallots spooned over. French fries and a green salad would be the classic accompaniment, but mashed potatoes also go well.

Simple Steak Sauce
Heat 1 tablespoon olive oil in a saucepan, add 110 g sliced shallots and cook until lightly browned. Add 125 ml red wine and 1 tablespoon balsamic vinegar, bring to the boil, then simmer for 10 minutes until reduced by three-quarters. Add 150 ml beef stock, simmer for 5 minutes, then strain, return to the pan and whisk in 1 teaspoon butter paste (equal parts soft butter and plain flour mixed to a smooth paste). Bring back to the boil and simmer until thickened. Season to taste with salt, pepper and a few drops of Worcestershire sauce.

The key thing to remember with this great French bistro classic is not to scorch the peppercorns, which will make the dish taste bitter. This means using a thin cut of steak and cooking it briefly in oil and butter, rather than searing it in a dry pan. Using Madeira in place of the traditional Cognac gives the sauce a mellow edge.

steak au poivre

1 tablespoon black or mixed peppercorns

2 entrecôte or rump steaks, 200–225 g each and 1.5 cm thick

1 tablespoon olive oil

15 g butter

50 ml medium-dry Madeira

75 ml beef stock

1 rounded tablespoon crème fraîche

tomato ketchup, to taste (optional)

sea salt

to serve

Classic French Fries (page 53) or Smooth, Creamy Mash (page 53)

green salad or steamed green beans

serves 2

Put the peppercorns in a mortar and crush roughly with a pestle. Trim the steaks of any excess fat and pat dry with kitchen paper. Lay them in a shallow dish, then sprinkle both sides with the ground peppercorns, reserving a little for the sauce. Cover and set aside for 30 minutes.

Heat a frying pan over medium heat and add the olive oil. When the oil is hot, add the butter, and once it has melted, add the steaks to the pan. Cook for about 2½ minutes, then turn over and cook for a further 1½ minutes for a rare steak. For a medium-rare steak, cook for 3 minutes on the first side and 2 minutes on the other. Transfer to a warm plate and cover lightly with aluminium foil.

Pour off the butter from the pan and add the Madeira. Let bubble up until it has almost evaporated. Add the beef stock and simmer until it has reduced by half. Remove the pan from the heat and stir in the crème fraîche. Season to taste with salt and a little of the remaining black pepper. If the sauce tastes bitter, add about ½ teaspoon tomato ketchup. Stir in any meat juices that have accumulated under the steak.

Serve the steaks on warm plates with the sauce spooned over. Accompany with French fries or mashed potatoes and a green salad or green beans.

The traditional cut to use for this classic Tuscan recipe, known locally as Bistecca alla Fiorentina, is a T-bone steak, marinated overnight in olive oil and garlic and cooked over a charcoal barbecue or an open fire. Alternatively, you could use a gas barbecue – either way it's a treat for any meat lover!

Tuscan-style steak

1 large T-bone steak, about 700 g and cut to an even thickness of 2.5–3 cm

100 ml olive oil

2 garlic cloves, thinly sliced

3 sprigs of rosemary

sea salt and freshly ground black pepper

good-quality extra virgin olive oil, for drizzling

to serve

sautéed potatoes

rocket salad

lemon wedges (optional)

serves 2

Trim the excess fat off the edge of the steak, leaving a little if liked, and pat the steak dry with kitchen paper. Pour the measured olive oil into a shallow dish and add the garlic and rosemary. Turn the steak in the oil, ensuring there is some garlic and rosemary on each side. Cover with a double layer of clingfilm and let marinate in the refrigerator for 24 hours, turning a couple of times. Bring to room temperature before cooking it.

Preheat a charcoal barbecue or build a good fire and let it burn until the flames have completely died down and the ash is a powdery white. Take the meat out of the marinade and remove any pieces of garlic or rosemary from the steak. Pat dry with kitchen paper. Put the steak on a rack about 8 cm above the coals and cook for about 4 minutes. Turn the steak over and cook for a further 3 minutes. (Cook for a couple of minutes longer on each side for a medium-rare steak, although this is traditionally served rare.)

Transfer to a warm plate and season both sides with salt and pepper. Cover lightly with aluminium foil, then let rest for 5 minutes.

Stand the steak upright with the bone at the bottom and, using a sharp knife, remove the meat either side of the bone in one piece. Cut the meat into slices, 0.5–1 cm thick. Divide the slices between 2 serving plates. Pour over any meat juices that have accumulated under the meat and drizzle with the best extra virgin olive oil you can lay your hands on.

Serve with sautéed potatoes, a rocket salad and lemon wedges, if liked, accompanied by a glass of Chianti Classico.

To my mind, béarnaise is the most delicious steak sauce ever. It is slightly tricky to handle, so I recommend making it in a food processor. You don't need any other sauce with the steak – just the meat juices.

grilled rib-eye steak
with béarnaise sauce

2–3 rib-eye steaks, about 225 g each and 3 cm thick

olive oil, for rubbing

béarnaise sauce

a handful of tarragon sprigs, leaves chopped, stalks reserved

3 tablespoons white wine vinegar

1 small shallot, chopped

6 black peppercorns

1 bay leaf

200 g unsalted butter

2 organic egg yolks

sea salt

to serve

lightly dressed watercress, spinach and rocket salad

Classic French Fries (page 53)

a ridged stove-top grill pan

serves 2–3

First, prepare the base for the béarnaise sauce. Put the tarragon stalks in a small saucepan and add the vinegar, shallot, peppercorns and the bay leaf. Bring to the boil, then simmer until you have just 1 tablespoon of liquid left. Strain it into a small bowl and let cool.

To cook the steaks, heat a ridged stove-top grill pan over high heat until almost smoking. Trim the steaks of any excess fat, pat dry with kitchen paper, then rub a little oil into both sides. Add them to the pan and cook for 2–3 minutes, depending whether you want them rare or medium-rare. When you see spots of blood rise to the surface, turn them over and cook on the other side for another 1½–2½ minutes – again, depending on whether you want them rare or medium-rare. Transfer to a warm plate and cover lightly with aluminium foil.

To make the béarnaise sauce, put the butter in a small saucepan with a lip and heat gently until melted. Skim off any white residue that floats to the surface, then bring almost to boiling point. Put the egg yolks in a food processor, add half the reduced vinegar and blend until the mixture begins to lighten and thicken. With the motor running, add the melted butter to the egg yolks through the feed tube very gradually, drip by drip. Once it begins to thicken, pour in the remaining butter in a steady stream. Stop pouring once you get to the milky residue at the bottom of the pan. Add the remaining reduced vinegar and a little salt and blend. Add the tarragon leaves and pulse a few times to incorporate. Taste and adjust the seasoning, if necessary.

Serve the steaks with the sauce spooned alongside, with a lightly dressed watercress, spinach and rocket salad and French fries.

I prefer this way of serving stroganoff to the traditional one that involves slicing the meat. Rump steak can be slightly tougher than other steak cuts, so make sure you buy from a reliable butcher and trim off any fat.

rump steak stroganoff

4 rump steaks, 150 g each and about 1.5 cm thick

2 tablespoons light olive oil

50 g butter

2–3 shallots, finely chopped

1 garlic clove, crushed

250 g chestnut mushrooms, wiped clean and sliced

2 teaspoons plain flour

1 teaspoon sweet pimentón (Spanish oak-smoked paprika)

1 tablespoon tomato purée

75 ml dry white wine

75 ml beef stock

150 ml sour cream

sea salt and coarsely ground black pepper

freshly squeezed lemon juice, to taste

scissor-snipped chives, to garnish

buttered fettucine or plain rice, to serve

serves 4

Trim the steaks of any excess fat and pat dry with kitchen paper. Heat a heavy frying pan over high heat, then add 1 tablespoon of the olive oil and, a few seconds later, a third of the butter. When the foaming has died down, add the steaks and sear for 2–3 minutes each side, depending whether you want them rare or medium-rare. Transfer to a warm plate and cover lightly with aluminium foil.

Meanwhile, pour the fat out of the pan, then replace the pan over low to medium heat and add the remaining olive oil and butter. When the butter has melted, fry the shallots for about 2 minutes, without colouring, then add the garlic and the mushrooms. Increase the heat and stir-fry for about 2 minutes until the mushrooms have softened. Stir in the flour, pimentón and tomato purée, then add the wine and beef stock. Reduce the heat and simmer for 2–3 minutes until the sauce is thick and reduced.

Take the pan off the heat and stir in the sour cream. Pour in any juices that have accumulated under the steaks and reheat gently without boiling. Add a squeeze of lemon juice and season with salt and pepper.

Serve the steaks with the sauce spooned over, garnished with black pepper and chives. Buttered fettucine or plain rice make good accompaniments.

This luxurious recipe, traditionally known as Tournedos Rossini, makes a very special dinner for two. I like this lighter version with sourdough toasts. It's quick and easy to make, but it's important to keep each component of the recipe warm as you cook it.

fillet steaks
with foie gras and truffles

4 small fillet steaks, 75–85 g each and 1.5 cm thick

1–2 fresh or preserved black truffles, about 40 g

3 teaspoons olive oil

40 g butter

2 long, thin slices of white sourdough bread

2 thick slices of fresh foie gras or 3 thin slices of preserved foie gras, about 80 g

4 tablespoons Madeira

4 tablespoons beef stock

sea salt and freshly ground black pepper

lightly cooked green beans, broccoli or spinach, to serve

serves 2

Take the steaks out of the refrigerator 1 hour before you intend to cook them. Trim of any excess fat or sinew and pat dry with kitchen paper. Thinly slice the truffles, reserving the best slices for the garnish, then finely chop the rest.

Heat a heavy frying pan over medium heat, add 1 teaspoon of the olive oil, then, when it has warmed through, add 10 g of the butter. Warm through the truffle slices for a few seconds on either side and set aside on a warm plate. Increase the heat, add another teaspoon of the olive oil and another 10 g butter and fry the slices of bread briefly on each side until crisp, then transfer to the plate with the truffles.

Add the remaining olive oil and another 10 g of the butter to the pan. Season the steaks lightly with salt and pepper and cook over medium heat for 3–4 minutes, turning regularly, depending on whether you want them rare or medium-rare. Transfer to a warm plate and cover lightly with aluminium foil.

Carefully lay the slices of foie gras in the pan and cook them for just a few seconds each side, then put them on the steak plate. Pour any remaining fat out of the pan then pour in the Madeira, let bubble up and reduce to about 1 tablespoon, then add the beef stock and chopped truffles. Simmer for a couple of minutes, then add the remaining butter and any juices that have accumulated under the steaks. To serve, take a couple of warm plates, put a slice of sourdough toast on each and place the sliced foie gras on top. Top with 2 slices of steak. Spoon over half the truffle sauce and top with the truffle slices. Serve with lightly cooked green beans, broccoli or spinach.

½ small-medium red onion, chopped

1 tablespoon capers, rinsed and chopped

3 small gherkins, rinsed and chopped

2–3 anchovy fillets, chopped

2 tablespoons chopped flat leaf parsley, plus extra leaves to garnish

300–325 g chilled fillet steak

2 tablespoons extra virgin olive oil, plus extra to serve

1 teaspoon Worcestershire sauce, plus extra to serve

a few drops of Tabasco sauce, plus extra to serve

¼ teaspoon finely grated lemon zest

flaked sea salt and freshly ground black pepper

to serve

tomato ketchup

lightly dressed salad leaves

Classic French Fries (page 53) or crostini*

**serves 2 as a main
or 4 as a starter**

It goes without saying that you need to choose your steak carefully for this classic raw dish. It needs to be tender and impeccably fresh – so not previously frozen or darkened through exposure to air. The tail end of fillet is the best cut to use, which is usually less expensive than prime fillet. There are many different ways of making steak tartare and this light, lemony version, using olive oil rather than the traditional egg yolk, is the way I like it. Purists say you should chop the meat by hand, but unless you have razor-sharp chefs' knives, it's easier to use a food processor.

steak tartare

Put the chopped onion, capers, gherkins, anchovy fillets and parsley on a chopping board and chop finely together until well mixed.

Trim the fillet steak of any excess fat and pat dry with kitchen paper. Cut into slices, then into small cubes. Put in a food processor and pulse 5–6 times, just enough to give you a coarse, clean cut – it mustn't get smooth or turn to a paste. Transfer to a bowl, add the chopped onion and caper mixture and mix together lightly with a fork. Add the olive oil, Worcestershire sauce and a few drops of Tabasco sauce and mix together. Add the lemon zest, some black pepper and a good pinch of salt flakes, rubbed between your fingers. Mix thoroughly.

Form into 2 or 4 burger-shaped patties, placing one on each plate. Drizzle a little olive oil around each patty and garnish with parsley leaves. Serve immediately accompanied by extra Worcestershire sauce and Tabasco sauce and some tomato ketchup. The traditional main course accompaniments are French fries and salad, but if you're serving it as a starter, I'd serve it with a few lightly dressed salad leaves and crostini.

*Note To make crostini, put 12 thin slices of ciabatta bread on a baking sheet and spray with olive oil. Bake in a preheated oven at 180 °C (350°F) Gas 4 for 15 minutes, turning once.

Argentinian-style 'asado' steak

with chimichurri salsa

a whole piece of sirloin, 1.5–1.75 kg

olive oil, for rubbing and brushing

sea salt

chimichurri salsa

150 ml olive oil

75 ml red wine vinegar

1 teaspoon dried oregano

4–5 tablespoons chopped flat leaf parsley, stalks removed and chopped

½–1 teaspoon crushed dried chillies

2 large garlic cloves, finely chopped

1 bay leaf

150 ml *salmuera* (salt water solution made from 1 rounded tablespoon sea salt dissolved in 150 ml warm water and cooled)

to serve

roasted new potatoes*

green salad

serves 8–10

In Argentina, they tend to cook steak in a whole piece over an open fire (*asado*). With their wonderful beef, it makes for a fabulous party treat. Serve it with the classic accompaniment of chimichurri salsa – a punchy, garlic dressing that needs to be made the day before for the flavours to fully develop.

To make the chimichurri salsa, put the olive oil, vinegar, oregano, parsley, crushed dried chillies, garlic, bay leaf and *salmuera* in a screw-top jar and shake well. Chill overnight in the refrigerator. Bring to room temperature before serving.

Trim the meat of excess fat, then rub lightly with olive oil and sprinkle with salt. Preheat a charcoal barbecue and let it burn until the flames have completely died down and the ash is a powdery white. Put the beef on a rack 8 cm above the hot coals. Cook for 15–20 minutes for a rare steak or 25–30 minutes for a medium-rare steak, turning every 4–5 minutes. If the meat seems to be drying out, brush over a little extra oil. Transfer to a warm plate, cover lightly with aluminium foil and let rest for 5–10 minutes.

Cut the steak into thick slices and serve a couple of slices on each plate. Shake the chimichurri salsa vigorously and splash over the steaks. Serve with roasted new potatoes and a green salad.

*Note To make roasted new potatoes, put 1 kg halved new potatoes in a roasting tin with 75 ml olive oil, 4 sprigs of rosemary and 6–8 garlic cloves. Roast in a preheated oven at 180°C (350°F) Gas 4 for about 45 minutes, turning occasionally.

contemporary steaks

Fillet steak provides a tasty alternative to tuna in this Provençal-inspired salad, which makes the perfect summer lunch.

steak niçoise

½ teaspoon coarse sea salt

1 teaspoon black peppercorns

1 teaspoon dried rosemary

400 g fillet steak

2 tablespoons olive oil

200 g fine green beans, trimmed

12 anchovy fillets

100 g rocket or mixed salad leaves

250 g cherry or mini plum tomatoes, halved

75 g black olives marinated in oil and herbs

milk, for soaking (optional)

basil leaves or finely chopped flat leaf parsley, to garnish

crusty bread or buttered new potatoes and chives, to serve

dressing

1 teaspoon Dijon mustard

2 tablespoons white wine vinegar

110 ml olive oil

sea salt and freshly ground black pepper

serves 4

Put the salt, peppercorns and rosemary in a mortar and pound with a pestle until finely ground. Trim the beef of any excess fat and pat dry with kitchen paper, then roll it in the ground salt, pepper and rosemary until evenly coated.

Heat a large frying pan over medium to high heat, add the olive oil then, once the oil is hot, lay the fillet in the pan. Cook on all sides for 5–6 minutes, turning every minute, depending on whether you want it rare or medium-rare. Set aside to cool, then cover and chill in the refrigerator for at least 1 hour.

Meanwhile, bring a saucepan of water to the boil and cook the green beans for 10 minutes. Rinse in cold water and drain.

Taste the anchovies, and if they are excessively salty, soak them in just enough milk to cover for 15 minutes. Drain and pat dry, then cut in half lengthways.

To make the dressing, put the mustard, vinegar and some salt and pepper in a bowl and whisk together. Gradually whisk in the olive oil until the dressing has a thick consistency.

Once the beef is well chilled, slice it thinly with a sharp knife. Assemble the salad on individual plates, starting with a layer of rocket, a few beans and some tomatoes. Next lay on the beef slices and anchovies. Give the dressing another whisk and spoon over the salad. Dot the olives and basil leaves around the salad. Serve with crusty bread or buttered new potatoes and chives.

Carpaccio is traditionally a raw steak dish, but I like this version where the meat is well seasoned and seared first. It makes a fabulous showy dinner party dish.

seared steak carpaccio
with truffle vinaigrette and rocket

500 g fillet steak of even thickness*

2 tablespoons mixed peppercorns

1 teaspoon herbes de Provence

2 tablespoons olive oil

100 g rocket leaves

truffle vinaigrette

2 tablespoons white wine vinegar

½ teaspoon balsamic vinegar

2 teaspoons white truffle-flavoured olive oil

6 tablespoons light olive oil

2 tablespoons whipping cream

sea salt and freshly ground black pepper

to serve

shavings of Parmesan cheese

crusty bread (optional)

serves 4 as a main or 6 as a starter

Trim the beef of any excess fat or sinew and pat dry with kitchen paper. Put the peppercorns in a mortar with the herbes de Provence and pound with a pestle until crushed. Coat all sides of the meat with the crushed peppercorns and herbs, wrap in clingfilm and chill in the refrigerator for 1 hour.

Heat a frying pan over medium to high heat for about 3 minutes until hot. Add the oil, heat for 1 minute, then brown the meat on all sides for 2–3 minutes, turning regularly to prevent the peppercorns burning. Set aside to cool, then rewrap the meat and put it in the freezer for about 45 minutes until firm.

To make the vinaigrette, put the vinegars in a bowl and season with salt and pepper. Whisk in the truffle oil and olive oil until the dressing is thick, then gradually add the cream. Taste and adjust the seasoning, if necessary, and set aside.

Slice the beef as thinly as you can with a very sharp knife and lay it between sheets of greaseproof paper. Beat it out with a meat mallet or rolling pin to make it thinner still.

Arrange the rocket leaves on each plate, then lay over the slices of carpaccio. Whisk the dressing again and spoon a little over each portion. Top with shavings of Parmesan and serve with crusty bread, if liked.

*Note It's important to buy a piece of meat of an even thickness so that it cooks evenly.

This recipe is a version of one I tried in a stunning restaurant called Le Quartier Français in Franschhoek. It makes the perfect dinner party dish and everyone will ask you for the recipe! Start preparing the meat two days in advance.

1 kg chateaubriand, cut in one piece from the centre of the fillet

2 tablespoons light olive oil

15 g butter

sugar cure

30 g coarse sea salt

1½ teaspoons black peppercorns

1½ teaspoons Szechuan peppercorns

1 tablespoon coriander seeds

1 garlic clove, chopped

1½ teaspoons herbes de Provence

50 g light muscovado sugar

50 g dark muscovado sugar

to serve

Simple Steak Sauce (page 12)

Parsnip Purée (see below) or Smooth, Creamy Mash (page 53)

lightly steamed, buttered vegetables, such as asparagus

serves 6

South African sugar-cured chateaubriand

To make the sugar cure, put the salt, peppercorns and coriander seeds in a mortar and pound with a pestle until coarsely ground. Add the garlic and herbes de Provence and pound again. Transfer to a large, shallow dish and stir in the sugars.

Trim the meat of any excess fat, pat dry with kitchen paper, then put in the dish and rub with the sugar cure. Cover with a double layer of clingfilm and chill in the refrigerator for 48 hours, turning occasionally. The moisture in the meat will dissolve the sugar, creating a rich marinade.

Rinse the sugar cure off the meat and pat dry with kitchen paper. Heat an ovenproof frying pan over high heat and add the olive oil. When the oil is hot, add the butter. When the butter has melted, add the meat and cook for about 5 minutes, turning, until well browned. Transfer the pan to a preheated oven and cook at 225°C (425°F) Gas 7 for 12–15 minutes for a rare steak and up to 20 minutes for a medium-rare steak. Transfer to a warm plate, cover lightly with aluminium foil and let rest for 5–10 minutes.

Carve the meat into medium-thick slices and put 2 or 3 slices on each plate. Serve with a spoonful of simple steak sauce, parsnip purée or mashed potatoes, and lightly steamed, buttered vegetables.

Parsnip Purée
Put 1 kg peeled, quartered, cored and chopped parsnips in a saucepan, cover with boiling water and cook for 15–20 minutes until tender. Drain, reserving the cooking water. Blend in a food processor with 25 g butter, 2 tablespoons crème fraîche and a little of the cooking water to make a smooth, slightly sloppy purée. Season well with salt, pepper and nutmeg.

This recipe is a great way of stretching a small amount of steak. You can of course use a commercial teriyaki marinade to save time.

teriyaki steak with noodles

350 g rump or sirloin steak, sliced about 1 cm thick

3 tablespoons sunflower or rapeseed oil

1 red pepper, quartered, cored and cut into strips

100 g shiitake mushrooms, rinsed and halved

100 g sugar snap peas

5–6 spring onions, trimmed and cut into 4 cm lengths

375 g dried egg noodles

sansho pepper or coarsely ground black pepper

marinade

4 tablespoons Japanese soy sauce

4 tablespoons sake

2 tablespoons mirin (Japanese rice wine)

1½ teaspoons unrefined caster sugar

1 garlic clove, crushed

serves 4

To make the marinade, mix the ingredients in a shallow bowl. Trim the steak of any excess fat or sinews and cut into strips about 1.5 cm wide. Toss the strips of steak in the marinade, then cover and set aside for 1 hour.

When ready to cook, remove the meat from the marinade and pat dry with kitchen paper. Heat a wok over high heat for a couple of minutes, add 1 tablespoon of the sunflower oil and swirl around the side. Add the meat and stir-fry briefly on both sides. Add a couple of tablespoons of the marinade and stir-fry for a few seconds more, then transfer to a warm plate.

Rinse the wok and dry with kitchen paper, then add the remaining oil and the pepper strips and stir-fry over high heat for 1 minute. Add the rest of the vegetables and stir-fry for another 3–4 minutes. Pour in the remaining marinade and let bubble up until the liquid has reduced by half. Add 50 ml water to prevent the sauce tasting too salty.

Put the steak back in the pan together with any juices that have accumulated under the meat, stir-fry for a few seconds, then turn off the heat.

Meanwhile, cook the noodles following the instructions on the packet, then drain. Divide between 4 deep bowls and spoon over the meat and vegetables. Sprinkle with sansho pepper.

This is an adaptation of what many consider the Korean national dish – a barbecued steak recipe called Bulgogi. I think it's easier to make in a wok, but you can barbecue the meat if you prefer.

Korean-style stir-fried steak
with garlic, soy and sesame

3 sirloin steaks, 225 g each and 2.5 cm thick

1 tablespoon sesame seeds

3 tablespoons vegetable oil

2 teaspoons sesame oil

a bunch of spring onions, trimmed and finely shredded

marinade

3 tablespoons tamari soy sauce

3 tablespoons unseasoned rice vinegar

2 tablespoons sesame oil

1 teaspoon hot pepper sauce

2 tablespoons unrefined caster sugar

2–4 garlic cloves, crushed

2 teaspoons finely grated ginger

to serve

Kimchee or cucumber pickle*

8 iceberg or Webbs lettuce leaves

sticky rice

serves 4

To make the marinade, mix the tamari with 50 ml water in a shallow dish. Add the rest of the marinade ingredients and whisk together with a fork. Trim the steak of excess fat, cut diagonally into pieces about 1 cm thick. Put in the marinade, cover and let marinate for 45 minutes to 1 hour.

If not using ready-made pickles, prepare your own (see below). Put the lettuce in a bowl of iced water. Dry-roast the sesame seeds in a frying pan for 4–5 minutes until lightly browned.

Remove the beef from the marinade and pat dry with kitchen paper. Mix the vegetable oil and sesame oil in a small bowl. Heat a wok over high heat until almost smoking, add 2 teaspoons of the mixed oil and swirl around the side. Lay a third of the beef slices in the wok. Cook for 1½ minutes, then flip and cook for another minute. Transfer to a warm serving plate, cover lightly with aluminium foil and set aside. Rinse the wok and dry with kitchen paper. Add another 2 teaspoons of the oil and fry the remaining meat in 2 batches. Wipe the wok with kitchen paper, add the remaining oil and fry the spring onions for about 1 minute until just wilted. Scatter over the steak and sprinkle with the toasted sesame seeds. Drain the lettuce leaves and pat dry with kitchen paper. Serve the steak rolled up in the lettuce leaves, with sticky rice and Kimchee.

*Note Kimchee is a pickled cabbage salad traditionally served with this dish. If unavailable, make your own cabbage pickle. Mix a jar of drained pickled red cabbage with some grated ginger and finely chopped chillies. To make cucumber pickle, peel a cucumber and cut in half lengthways. Scoop out the seeds and cut into thin slices. Sprinkle with salt, cover with a weighted plate and let stand for 20 minutes. Rinse the cucumber and mix with a little rice vinegar and some finely chopped, deseeded red chilli.

1 tablespoon Thai fragrant rice

¼ teaspoon crushed dried chillies (optional)

1 rump steak, 400–450 g and about 2 cm thick

1 tablespoon sunflower oil or light olive oil

dressing

1½–2 teaspoons unrefined caster sugar

freshly squeezed juice of 2 limes

1 large garlic clove, crushed

2 tablespoons Thai fish sauce

4 small shallots, very thinly sliced, or 3–4 spring onions, thinly sliced

1–2 medium-hot fresh red chillies, deseeded and thinly sliced

3 rounded tablespoons coriander leaves, chopped

2 rounded tablespoons mint leaves, chopped

125 g cherry tomatoes, quartered

mixed salad leaves, to serve

a ridged stove-top grill pan

serves 3–4

Thailand is home to some great meat-based salads that are wonderfully zingy and refreshing. The amount of chilli you use is up to you. You can omit the dry-roasted chillies and only use fresh ones, but I like the smoky flavour they add to the dish.

Thai-style steak and tomato salad

Heat a small saucepan over medium heat, add the rice and cook, stirring occasionally, until golden and fragrant – about 5 minutes. Remove from the heat, let cool for a couple of minutes, then grind in a mortar with a pestle. Dry-roast the crushed dried chillies, if using, in another small saucepan over medium heat for about 1 minute, add to the rice and grind again.

Trim the steak of any excess fat and pat dry with kitchen paper. Heat a ridged stove-top grill pan over high heat until it begins to smoke – about 3–4 minutes, then rub the steak with the oil and cook for about 1½ minutes each side until charred, but still rare. Transfer to a plate and let cool.

To make the dressing, put the sugar and lime juice in a large bowl and stir until dissolved. Add the garlic, fish sauce and 2 tablespoons water. Add any juices that have accumulated under the steak, then mix in the shallots, fresh chilli, coriander, mint and tomatoes.

Scatter some mixed salad leaves on a large serving plate, place the steak on top and pour over the dressing. Sprinkle with the toasted rice. Thinly slice the steak to serve.

2 tablespoons vegetable oil or other cooking oil

1 large onion, chopped

2 cm fresh ginger, peeled and finely chopped

1 garlic clove, crushed

1 small red chilli, deseeded and thinly sliced

1.5 litres beef stock

1 tablespoon hoisin sauce, or to taste

2–3 tablespoons Asian fish sauce

3–4 tablespoons freshly squeezed lime or lemon juice

250 g medium dried rice noodles

175 g lean rump steak

sea salt and freshly ground black pepper

Tabasco sauce, to taste

to serve

4 spring onions, trimmed and thinly sliced

125 g fresh beansprouts

coriander leaves

mint leaves

1–2 red chillies, thinly sliced

1 lime or lemon, cut into wedges

serves 4

This addictive Vietnamese noodle dish is pronounced 'fer' rather than, as you'd assume, 'fo'. As it is cooked very quickly, it benefits from a tender cut of steak, although you will need a relatively small amount.

Vietnamese pho

Heat the oil in a large saucepan and fry the onion over medium heat until browned – about 8–10 minutes. Add the ginger, garlic and chilli, stir, then pour in the stock. Add the hoisin sauce, fish sauce and lime juice, stir, then leave the stock to simmer on low heat while you prepare the accompaniments.

Plunge the noodles into a saucepan of boiling, salted water, bring back to the boil, making sure they don't stick together, and cook for 1 minute. Drain and rinse under cold water.

Trim any fat off the steak and slice it as thinly as you possibly can, cutting the larger slices into strips. Add the meat to the hot stock and season lightly with salt and pepper and taste. If you think it needs spicing up, add a bit more hoisin and/or Tabasco sauce. To sharpen the flavour, add more fish sauce or lemon juice.

Divide the noodles between 4 deep bowls, top with the spring onions and beansprouts and ladle over the hot stock. Sprinkle with coriander and mint. Serve with little dishes of sliced chillies, Tabasco sauce and lime wedges so that people can adjust the seasoning if they wish.

sandwiches and wraps

I love the combination of steak and melting, gooey blue cheese. Here I've used mature Stilton, but you could equally well use Gorgonzola.

toasted steak, stilton and watercress sandwich

60 g mature blue Stilton, rind removed

25 g butter, softened

a small pinch of cayenne pepper or paprika

225 g thinly sliced minute steak

1 tablespoon olive oil

1 medium ciabatta loaf

a small handful of watercress

sea salt and freshly ground black pepper

balsamic dressing

1 teaspoon balsamic vinegar

3 teaspoons light olive oil

sea salt and freshly ground black pepper

a ridged stove-top grill pan (optional)

serves 2

To make the balsamic dressing, mix the vinegar and olive oil in a small bowl, then season with salt and pepper. Set aside.

Mash the Stilton with the butter and season with the cayenne pepper. Heat a ridged stove-top grill pan or a frying pan over high heat until very hot. Rub the slices of steak lightly with the olive oil and season with salt and pepper. Sear for 1 minute each side, then set aside.

Cut the ciabatta in half crossways, then in half lengthways. Briefly toast the outside of the bottom halves under a preheated hot grill, then turn them over and pile on the steak slices and dot with the Stilton butter. Grill for about 1 minute until the cheese melts, then transfer to warm plates.

Lightly toast the outside of the remaining halves of ciabatta. Place a few watercress leaves on top of the Stilton butter and drizzle with the balsamic dressing, then cover with the remaining ciabatta halves. Serve immediately.

A delicious twist on a steak sandwich. It is simple to make if you have an electric grilling machine, but it can be easily adapted if you haven't (see below).

steak, pepper and pecorino panini

4 minute steaks, 0.5 cm thick, 350 g in total

5 tablespoons garlic-flavoured olive oil

1 onion, thickly sliced

1 large red pepper or ½ red pepper and ½ yellow pepper, quartered, cored and sliced

10–12 basil leaves, torn

100 g pecorino cheese, thinly sliced

4 panini or ciabatta rolls

sea salt and freshly ground black pepper

an electric grilling machine (optional)

serves 4

Trim the steaks of any excess fat and pat dry with kitchen paper. Put 2 tablespoons of the oil in a shallow dish. Add the steaks, rub in the oil and season with black pepper. Heat a frying pan and add the remaining oil. Add the onion and pepper and stir-fry over medium heat until beginning to brown. Remove the pan from the heat, stir in the basil leaves and season lightly with salt and pepper.

Heat an electric grilling machine to its maximum setting and cook the steaks for about 1 minute, in batches, if necessary. Set aside to rest on a warm plate. Wipe the grill with some kitchen paper to remove any burnt-on meat juices.

Split open the rolls, lay a piece of steak on the bottom halves, top with the fried onions and peppers and cover with slices of pecorino. Put the top halves of the rolls on top and place the filled panini on the grill. Press down the lid and cook for another minute. Remove from the grilling machine, then cut in half and serve immediately.

Note If you haven't got an electric grilling machine, sear the steak in a frying pan or ridged stove-top grill pan, then put in toasted paninis with the onion, pepper, basil and pecorino, like the Toasted Steak, Stilton and Watercress Sandwich (page 43).

sourdough steak sandwich
with tomato, rocket and homemade pesto

2 large medium-thick slices of sourdough or other country bread

75 g thinly sliced cooked steak, preferably rare

1 tomato, sliced

a handful of rocket leaves or mixed rocket salad

sea salt and freshly ground black pepper

pesto

50 g mature Parmesan cheese, rind removed

50 g pine nuts

1 small garlic clove, very finely chopped

2 large handfuls of basil leaves

75 ml good-quality extra virgin olive oil, plus extra to drizzle

½ teaspoon freshly squeezed lemon juice

sea salt and freshly ground black pepper

serves 1

In the – admittedly unlikely – event that you have some steak left over from barbecuing a large joint of meat, like the Argentinian-style 'Asado' Steak (page 27), here's what to do with it. Although you can buy very good fresh pesto from delicatessens nowadays, it's incredibly easy to make your own, and any leftovers will make a fabulous pasta sauce.

To make the pesto, crumble the Parmesan, breaking it up with a knife, if necessary, and put it in a food processor. Add the pine nuts and garlic and pulse in short bursts until the mixture is the consistency of large breadcrumbs. Add the basil and process briefly, then gradually add about 60 ml of the olive oil until you have a thick paste. Transfer to a bowl, add the lemon juice and some extra olive oil, if you think it needs it, then season with salt and pepper.

Lay out the 2 pieces of bread. Spread the base of one piece with a good dollop of pesto, lay over 3 or 4 slices of steak, top with the tomato and season lightly with salt and pepper. Put the rocket leaves on top and drizzle over a little olive oil. Press the top piece of bread down firmly and cut the sandwich in half.

Indian-spiced steak strips
with naan and cucumber raita

400 g minute steak, cut into thick strips

2–3 tablespoons sunflower oil

1 large onion, thinly sliced

1 teaspoon cumin seeds

2 large or 4 small naan breads

mango chutney, to serve (optional)

marinade

1 large garlic clove, chopped

½ teaspoon coarse or fine sea salt

1½ teaspoons garam masala

1½ teaspoons freshly squeezed lemon juice

3 tablespoons low-fat natural yoghurt

2 tablespoons sunflower oil

cucumber raita

½ cucumber, thinly sliced

150 ml low-fat natural yoghurt

1 tablespoon finely chopped mint

1 tablespoon finely chopped coriander, plus extra leaves to garnish

2–3 teaspoons freshly squeezed lemon juice

a pinch of garam masala

sea salt

serves 4

This strikingly different steak dish tastes like a spicy pizza. One to try out on your more adventurous friends.

To make the marinade, crush the garlic with the salt until it forms a paste. Add the garam masala, lemon juice and yoghurt and mix thoroughly, then stir in the sunflower oil. Put the steak strips in a bowl and pour over the marinade. Cover and let marinate for about 30 minutes.

Meanwhile, to make the cucumber raita, put the cucumber slices on a plate and lightly salt. Put a weighted plate on top and set aside for 15 minutes to disgorge (remove the bitter juices). Mix the yoghurt with the mint, coriander, lemon juice and garam masala. When the cucumber is ready, rinse and pat it dry, and add to the yoghurt mixture.

Heat a frying pan and add 2 tablespoons of the oil. Add the onion and fry over high heat for 3–4 minutes until well browned. Add the cumin seeds at the last minute and fry for a few seconds until they turn dark brown. Scoop out the onions and cumin seeds, transfer to a plate and set aside.

Remove the steak from the marinade, shaking off any excess. Add a little more oil to the frying pan, add the steak, a few pieces at a time, and fry for about 1 minute each side. Add more oil, if necessary. Transfer the steak strips to a warm plate and lightly cover with aluminium foil.

Lightly toast the naan breads. Put a small naan or half a large naan on each plate. Top with the steak strips and onions and spoon over any juices that have accumulated under the meat. Serve the cucumber raita alongside with some mango chutney, if liked. Decorate with a few coriander leaves.

2 long, thin pieces of bavette (skirt steak), about 175–200 g each, or 350–400 g minute steak

8 flour tortillas

crisp cos lettuce leaves, shredded

marinade

3 tablespoons freshly squeezed lime juice

1 garlic clove, crushed

1 teaspoon mild chilli powder

3 tablespoons light olive oil or sunflower oil

guacamole

2 large avocados, about 200 g each

2 tablespoons freshly squeezed lime juice

4 spring onions, trimmed and thinly sliced

1 garlic clove, crushed

1 small green chilli, deseeded and thinly sliced (optional)

1 tablespoon olive oil

2–3 tomatoes, about 175 g, skinned, deseeded and chopped

3 tablespoons chopped coriander leaves

sea salt

serves 4

The word fajitas, meaning straps, actually refers to the cut of beef that is traditionally used for this classic Tex-Mex dish, which is cooked over an open fire. If you want to use the authentic cut, you'll probably need to order it from a butcher.

char-grilled steak fajitas
with chunky guacamole

To make the marinade, put the lime juice, garlic and chilli powder in a shallow dish and whisk together. Gradually whisk in the olive oil. Put the steaks in the marinade and turn so that they are thoroughly coated. Cover and let marinate for 30 minutes while you prepare and light the barbecue.

Meanwhile, to make the guacamole, scoop out the flesh from the avocados and put it in a bowl with the lime juice. Chop with a knife to give a chunky consistency. Add the spring onions, garlic, chilli, if using, and olive oil and mix well. Add the tomatoes, coriander and salt, cover and set aside.

When the barbecue flames have completely died down and ash is a powdery white, pat the steak dry with kitchen paper and cook for about 1½ minutes each side. Set aside and let rest for 3–4 minutes while you warm the tortillas in a dry frying pan. Thinly slice the steak, then put a dollop of guacamole on each tortilla and top with slices of steak and shredded lettuce leaves. Carefully roll up the tortillas, press together and cut in half diagonally.

Note If you don't want to light a barbecue, you can cook the steak on a hot ridged stove-top grill pan or in a frying pan.

on the side

classic French fries

The secret of making really good chips is to fry them twice – once at a low temperature, then at a higher temperature to crisp them up. Always use good-quality, recently bought potatoes that are recommended for making chips. You really will notice the difference.

400 g chipping potatoes, such as Maris Piper, peeled and cut lengthways into quarters

vegetable oil, for deep-frying

coarse sea salt

a deep-fryer

serves 2

Cut each potato quarter into thin, even-sized chips, putting them in cold water as you go.

Fill a deep-fryer with oil to the manufacturer's recommended level and heat to 150°C (300°F). Dry the chips in a clean tea towel and put them in the frying basket (you may need to do this in batches if you have a small deep-fryer). Lower the basket into the hot oil and fry for 5 minutes without colouring. Remove, transfer to a roasting tin and set aside.

Once your steak is cooked and resting, increase the temperature of the oil to 190°C (375°F). Return the chips to the basket and fry for another 4–5 minutes until crisp and brown. Transfer to a bowl lined with kitchen paper and sprinkle lightly with salt, then shake well.

smooth, creamy mash

Because steak tends to be served simply with a butter or some sauce, it works best with the smoother, slightly sloppier mash that the French call 'purée' rather than the traditional British-style mash.

600 g waxy boiling potatoes, such as Desirée, peeled and quartered

50 ml whole milk

2 tablespoons double cream

50 g unsalted butter, cut into cubes, then softened

sea salt and freshly ground black pepper

serves 2–3

Put the potatoes in a saucepan and pour over enough boiling water to cover. Add 1 teaspoon of salt, bring to the boil, then reduce the heat and simmer gently for 12–15 minutes until you can pierce the potatoes easily with a skewer. Drain, then return to the saucepan and warm over very low heat for 1–2 minutes to dry off.

Mix the milk and cream together in a bowl and heat to just below boiling point in a microwave. Alternatively, heat in a small saucepan.

Cut the potatoes roughly with a knife, then mash thoroughly with a potato masher or a fork to remove any lumps. Work in the butter, then gradually beat in the warm milk and cream. Season to taste with salt and pepper.

spiced onion rings

These deliciously crispy, spicy onion rings make a good alternative to chips.

1 large Spanish onion, thickly sliced

125 g plain flour

½ teaspoon fine sea salt,
plus extra to serve

½ teaspoon bicarbonate of soda

1½ teaspoons cumin seeds

1 egg, lightly beaten

200 ml buttermilk, chilled

rapeseed or corn oil, for deep-frying

a deep-fryer

serves 3–4

Separate the larger onion rings and soak in iced water for 1 hour. Discard the smaller centre pieces. Fill a deep-fryer with oil to the manufacturer's recommended level and heat to 180°C (350°F). Sift the flour, salt and bicarbonate of soda into a bowl, mix in the cumin seeds and form a hollow in the middle. Mix the egg and buttermilk together, then pour half the mixture into the bowl, beat until smooth, then gradually add the rest.

Dry the onion rings with a clean tea towel. Dip a few rings in the batter, then hook them out with a fork, shake off any excess batter and drop into the hot oil. Fry for about 1½ minutes, turning once, until nicely browned. Using a slotted spoon, transfer to a baking dish and keep warm in a preheated low oven at 100°C (200°F). Repeat with the remaining rings. Sprinkle with salt and serve.

Provençal-style roast tomatoes

Perfect with simply grilled or pan-fried steak, these Provençal-style tomatoes look as good as they taste.

20 g dried breadcrumbs

10 g finely grated
Parmesan cheese

1 garlic clove, very finely chopped

2 tablespoons finely
chopped parsley

4 tablespoons extra virgin olive oil

400 g fresh pomodorino or
other small plum tomatoes,
halved lengthways

freshly ground black pepper

serves 3–4

Mix the breadcrumbs, Parmesan, garlic and parsley in a bowl and season with black pepper.

Put a little of the olive oil and 2 tablespoons water in a shallow dish. Lay the tomatoes, cut side up, in a single layer in the dish. Sprinkle over the breadcrumb mixture and drizzle with the remaining olive oil. Bake in a preheated oven at 180°C (350°F) Gas 4 for about 45 minutes or until the tomatoes are soft and the topping well browned.

creamed spinach

It's worth making this classic steakhouse side dish a couple of hours in advance to allow the flavours to infuse.

500 g fresh spinach

40 g butter

2 shallots, very finely chopped

125 ml double cream

¼ teaspoon freshly grated nutmeg

sea salt and freshly ground black pepper

freshly squeezed lemon juice, to taste

serves 3–4

Wash the spinach thoroughly and remove the thicker stalks. Put it in a saucepan without any extra water and heat over low heat, turning a couple of times, until the leaves collapse. Drain well, squeeze to remove any remaining liquid and chop roughly.

Warm the butter in a saucepan over low heat and add the shallots. Cook for about 5 minutes until soft, then add the spinach and turn thoroughly in the butter. Cook for 3–4 minutes, then add the cream and heat through. Season well with the nutmeg, some salt and pepper and a good squeeze of lemon juice. When ready to serve, reheat briefly.

portobello mushrooms with garlic and parsley butter

Steak, garlic and mushrooms have a wonderful affinity. You need the big, flavoursome portobello ones for this recipe.

85 g butter, softened

2 garlic cloves, crushed

3 rounded tablespoons finely chopped parsley

2 tablespoons olive oil

4 large or 8 medium portobello mushrooms, wiped and stalks trimmed

sea salt and freshly ground black pepper

serves 4

Put the butter in a bowl and mash it with the garlic and parsley, then season with salt and pepper.

Put 1 tablespoon of the olive oil in a baking dish large enough to contain the mushrooms in a single layer. Place the mushrooms in the dish, under-sides upwards. Divide the garlic butter between the mushrooms, spreading it evenly inside the cups. Drizzle the remaining olive oil over the edges of the mushrooms, then bake in a preheated oven at 200°C (400°F) Gas 6 for 30 minutes or until cooked through.

sauces and salsas

creamy gorgonzola sauce

An incredibly easy sauce that makes a sinfully good topping for steak.

150 g mild Gorgonzola, dolcelatte or similar creamy blue cheese, cut into cubes

75–90 ml whipping cream

freshly ground black pepper

freshly squeezed lemon juice, to taste

finely chopped parsley, to garnish

serves 4

Put the Gorgonzola in a bowl and mash it with 2 tablespoons of the cream. Tip the mixture into a small saucepan and heat gently, stirring occasionally, until the cheese has melted. Add another 3–4 tablespoons of cream until it achieves a sauce-like consistency. Check the seasoning, adding black pepper and a little lemon juice, if you think it needs it.

Serve the sauce poured over a steak and sprinkle with parsley.

aïoli

This classic mayonnaise can be made in a food processor, but it's easy to do by hand.

2–3 large fresh garlic cloves, chopped*

½ teaspoon flaked or coarse sea salt

¼ teaspoon mild chilli powder or sweet pimentón (Spanish oak-smoked paprika)

1 fresh organic egg yolk, at room temperature

75 ml fruity extra virgin olive oil, such as Provençal or Spanish

75 ml sunflower oil

¼ teaspoon wine vinegar

ground white or black pepper

serves 4

Put the garlic and salt in a mortar and pound to a smooth paste. Mix in the pimentón and egg yolk.

Pour the oils into a jug, then gradually drip into the egg and garlic mixture, pounding rhythmically and moving the pestle in the same direction. Continue until the mixture begins to stiffen and you hear a slapping noise as the oil goes in. Add the vinegar, then pour in the remaining oil in a steady, fine stream, stirring. Add 1–2 teaspoons warm water, ½ teaspoon at a time, to loosen the mixture. Season to taste with ground white pepper.

*Note Do not use garlic that has sprouted as this will make the aïoli taste bitter.

corn and pepper salsa

A great accompaniment for barbecued steak.

2 large corn cobs

3 tablespoons sunflower oil

4 spring onions, trimmed and thinly sliced

freshly squeezed juice of 1 lime

6 Pepperdew peppers, finely chopped

2 tablespoons finely chopped coriander leaves

a dash of chilli sauce or a large pinch of mild chilli powder (optional)

sea salt and freshly ground black pepper

serves 4

Holding the corn cobs upright, cut down the sides with a sharp knife to remove the kernels. Heat a large frying pan over medium heat and add 2 teaspoons of the oil. Stir-fry the corn for 2–3 minutes until it begins to brown. Add the spring onions and stir-fry for 1 minute. Transfer to a bowl and let cool for 10 minutes.

Add the lime juice, peppers, coriander and the remaining oil, and mix well. Add a dash of chilli sauce, if using, and season with salt and pepper.

salsa verde

This Italian-style salsa goes very well with a simply grilled rare steak.

4 rounded tablespoons finely chopped flat leaf parsley

1 rounded tablespoon finely chopped mint leaves

2 rounded tablespoons finely chopped basil leaves

100 ml extra virgin olive oil

3 spring onions, trimmed and finely chopped

2 garlic cloves, very finely chopped

2 tablespoons capers, rinsed and finely chopped

2 tablespoons gherkins, rinsed and finely chopped

3 anchovy fillets, finely chopped

2 teaspoons Dijon mustard mixed with 2 tablespoons red wine vinegar

freshly ground black pepper

serves 4–6

Put the herbs in a bowl with half the olive oil. Stir, add the spring onions, garlic, capers, gherkins and anchovy fillets and mix well. Add the mustard and vinegar mixture, then add enough olive oil to make the salsa slightly sloppy. Season to taste with black pepper.

fresh tomato salsa

This Mexican classic is delicious with barbecued steak or fajitas (page 51).

500 g ripe tomatoes, skinned and finely diced

½ red onion, finely chopped

1–2 small green chillies, deseeded and finely chopped

3 tablespoons freshly squeezed lime juice

a pinch of caster sugar

2 tablespoons finely chopped coriander

sea salt

serves 4

Put the tomatoes in a large bowl with the onion and chillies. Add the lime juice and mix well, then add the sugar and season with salt. When ready to serve, add the coriander.

steak butters

Flavoured butters can be made in advance and kept in the refrigerator to provide a delicious instant steak topping. Serve cool rather than chilled so that they melt on contact with the meat. All recipes serve 6.

lemon, garlic and parsley butter

1 garlic clove, chopped

¼ teaspoon fine sea salt

125 g unsalted butter, softened

1 tablespoon freshly squeezed lemon juice

½ teaspoon finely grated lemon zest

3 tablespoons finely chopped parsley

freshly ground black pepper

Put the garlic and salt in a mortar and crush with a pestle to a smooth paste.

Beat the butter with a wooden spoon or an electric hand-held mixer until light and smooth, then gradually work in the lemon juice. Add the garlic paste, lemon zest and parsley and beat thoroughly. Season with a little black pepper.

Spoon the flavoured butter onto a piece of aluminium foil and shape it into a rectangle. Roll up the foil into a sausage shape and twist the ends like a Christmas cracker, then chill until firm. Remove from the refrigerator 20–30 minutes before serving. Cut into thin slices and place 1 or 2 slices on each steak.

red wine and rosemary butter

75 ml full-bodied fruity red wine

a slice of red onion

1 bay leaf

¼ teaspoon tomato purée

125 g unsalted butter, softened

1 tablespoon finely chopped rosemary leaves

flaked sea salt and freshly ground black pepper

Put the wine, onion and bay leaf in a small saucepan, bring to the boil, then simmer for 7–8 minutes until reduced by two-thirds. Remove from the heat, stir in the tomato purée and let cool.

Beat the butter with a wooden spoon or an electric hand-held mixer until light and smooth, then gradually add the reduced wine. Stir in the rosemary and season with pepper and salt flakes, rubbed between your fingers.

Spoon the flavoured butter onto a piece of aluminium foil and shape it into a rectangle. Roll up the foil into a sausage shape and twist the ends like a Christmas cracker, then chill until firm. Remove from the refrigerator 20–30 minutes before serving. Cut into thin slices and place 1 or 2 slices on each steak.

blue cheese, cracked pepper and chive butter

100 g creamy blue cheese, such as Gorgonzola, Fourme d'Ambert or Cashel Blue

100 g unsalted butter, softened

1 teaspoon black peppercorns, crushed

1 rounded tablespoon finely snipped chives

Cut the butter and cheese into chunks, removing any rind from the cheese, and put in a bowl. Beat together with a wooden spoon or an electric hand-held mixer, then add the crushed peppercorns and the chives and mix thoroughly.

Spoon the flavoured butter onto a piece of aluminium foil and shape it into a rectangle. Roll up the foil into a sausage shape and twist the ends like a Christmas cracker, then chill until firm. Remove from the refrigerator 20–30 minutes before serving. Cut into thin slices and place 1 or 2 slices on each steak.

chilli, lime and coriander butter

110 g unsalted butter, softened

1 tablespoon freshly squeezed lime juice

2 garlic cloves, crushed

2 small red chillies, deseeded and very finely chopped

1 teaspoon finely grated lime zest

¼ teaspoon sweet pimentón (Spanish oak-smoked paprika)

1½ tablespoons finely chopped coriander leaves

flaked sea salt

Beat the butter with a wooden spoon or an electric hand-held mixer until light and smooth, then gradually work in the lime juice. Add the garlic, chillies, lime zest, pimentón, coriander and a good pinch of salt flakes, rubbed between your fingers.

Spoon the flavoured butter onto a piece of aluminium foil and shape it into a rectangle. Roll up the foil into a sausage shape and twist the ends like a Christmas cracker, then chill until firm. Remove from the refrigerator 20–30 minutes before serving. Cut into thin slices and place 1 or 2 slices on each steak.

index